SCHOLASTIC

40

CROSS-NUMBER PUZZLES

Fractions, Decimals & Percents

BY BOB OLENYCH

New York • Toronto • London • Auckland • Sydney **Teaching**
Mexico City • New Delhi • Hong Kong • Buenos Aires *Resources*

To all the students who enjoy the fun and challenge of math.

Cover design by Maria Lilja
Cover illustration by Dave Clegg
Interior design by Melinda Belter

ISBN 0-439-51906-3

3 4 5 6 7 8 9 10   40   11 10 09 08 07 06

40
CROSS-NUMBER PUZZLES
CONTENTS

40
CROSS-NUMBER PUZZLES
INTRODUCTION

FRACTIONS, DECIMALS, AND PERCENTS PRACTICE CAN BE FUN!

If fluency and accuracy are the goals you have established for your students learning fractions, decimals, and percents, then they should partake in regular review and practice with these skills. The key to motivating students is to provide them with a variety of activities that are interesting and stimulating. To support my students as they gain fluency and accuracy, I have created skill-building practice puzzles that they really enjoy.

WHAT YOU'LL FIND IN THIS BOOK

This book offers a collection of 40 fraction, decimal, and percent activities for a broad range of skills and abilities. The puzzles begin with fractions, then progress to decimals and percents. Within each skill, they are arranged from easy to difficult. You can match the needs of your students and target a specific skill by checking the detailed skill description listed both in the Table of Contents and on each activity page.

While many of the activities address a broad range of skills, some highlights of this book include the activities that reinforce two skills—expressing written numbers first as fractions, then as decimals. For example, one problem might read "twenty-six and thirteen thousandths." Students must first express this as a fraction, then as a decimal. Next, students must use the decimal answer to complete the cross-number puzzle. You can assign this type of activity at any time during the school year once the concepts have been taught, as it serves as an excellent review of these skills.

HOW TO USE THIS BOOK

Be sure to use these puzzles in a way that best suits the needs of your class. You may find it helpful to assign certain puzzles as practice work to follow a lesson, as in-class review work, or as homework. Where necessary, be sure to remind students that if they need more room to compute, they can use the back of the sheet or a piece of scrap paper—depending on your class policy. Whether they are solving a riddle or determining the missing numerator or denominator, students are motivated to check each problem so that they can finish the puzzle successfully.

CONNECTIONS TO THE MATH STANDARDS

Most of the puzzles in this book target NCTM 2000 objectives listed under the Number and Operations standard. These objectives include understanding ways to represent numbers, determining meanings of operations and how they relate to one another, and computing with fluency and accuracy. This book is packed with exercises that require students to use fractions, decimals, and percents in a variety of formats.

I am confident that your students, like mine, will enjoy this collection of puzzles and reap the benefits of practicing these essential skills.

Bob Olenych

CROSS-NUMBER 1 PUZZLE

FINDING THE VALUE OF A NUMERATOR OR DENOMINATOR Rename the mixed number to create an improper fraction. Find the missing numerator or denominator. Complete the puzzle by spelling out your answer in the appropriate across and down positions.

ACROSS

1. $3 \frac{5}{7} = 2 \frac{12}{}$

4. $5 \frac{1}{4} = 4 \frac{}{4}$

5. $9 \frac{2}{4} = 8 \frac{}{4}$

7. $2 \frac{11}{50} = 1 \frac{61}{}$

9. $2 \frac{5}{9} = 1 \frac{}{9}$

11. $2 \frac{5}{14} = 1 \frac{}{14}$

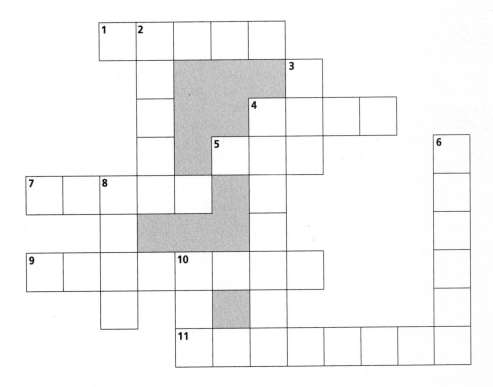

DOWN

2. $3 \frac{5}{8} = 2 \frac{13}{}$

3. $4 \frac{3}{6} = 3 \frac{9}{}$

4. $5 \frac{4}{11} = 4 \frac{}{11}$

6. $4 \frac{3}{8} = 3 \frac{}{8}$

8. $6 \frac{2}{4} = 5 \frac{6}{}$

10. $9 \frac{3}{7} = 8 \frac{}{7}$

NAME _____ DATE _____

CROSS-NUMBER
2
PUZZLE

FINDING THE LCD   Determine the LCD (Least Common Denominator) for each pair of fractions. Complete the puzzle by spelling out your answer in the appropriate across and down positions.

ACROSS

1. ⅓ and 2/7

3. ⅝ and ⅖

5. 6/9 and ⅔

6. ⅝ and ½

8. 2/4 and ⅕

10. 5/16 and ¾

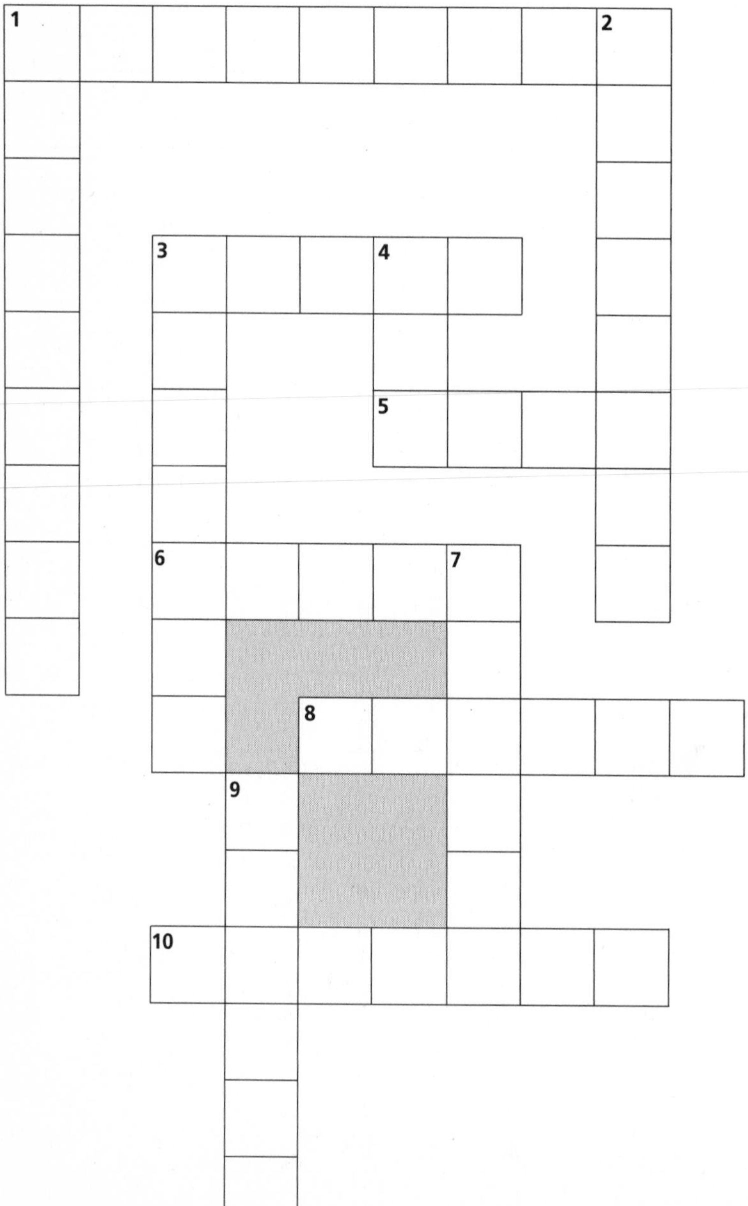

DOWN

1. ¾ and 4/9

2. ⅙ and 3/9

3. ⅓ and ⅖

4. ½ and ⅖

7. ⅓ and ¾

9. 2/6 and ⅕

40 CROSS-NUMBER PUZZLES: FRACTIONS, DECIMALS & PERCENTS • SCHOLASTIC TEACHING RESOURCES

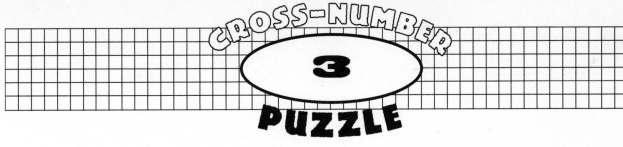

EXPRESSING ANSWERS IN LOWEST TERMS

Express all of the fractions below in their lowest terms. Complete the puzzle by spelling out the missing denominator in the appropriate across and down positions.

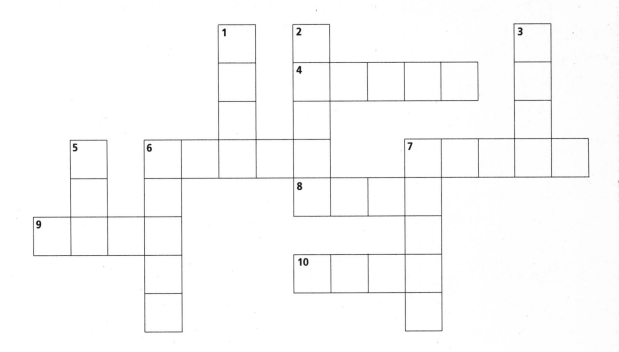

ACROSS

4. $^{10}/_{16} = {}^{5}/$

6. $^{10}/_{15} = {}^{2}/$

7. $^{12}/_{14} = {}^{6}/$

8. $^{14}/_{18} = {}^{7}/$

9. $^{3}/_{12} = {}^{1}/$

10. $^{6}/_{27} = {}^{2}/$

DOWN

1. $^{9}/_{12} = {}^{3}/$

2. $^{9}/_{21} = {}^{3}/$

3. $^{4}/_{20} = {}^{1}/$

5. $^{16}/_{32} = {}^{1}/$

6. $^{6}/_{18} = {}^{1}/$

7. $^{18}/_{21} = {}^{6}/$

NAME _____ DATE _____

CROSS-NUMBER
4
PUZZLE

ADDING MIXED FRACTIONS; UNLIKE DENOMINATORS; LOWEST TERMS Solve the problems below. Remember to express all answers in their lowest terms. Write your answers in the appropriate across and down positions.

 The fraction part of the mixed number should go in its own square.

ACROSS

2. $8\frac{4}{9} + 3\frac{2}{6} =$

3. $3\frac{1}{2} + 4\frac{6}{8} =$

4. $\frac{2}{6} + \frac{2}{3} + \frac{1}{2} =$

5. $4\frac{1}{3} + 6\frac{3}{4} =$

6. $\frac{1}{2} + 1\frac{5}{9} + \frac{5}{9} =$

DOWN

1. $3\frac{4}{18} + \frac{1}{3} + 9\frac{2}{9} =$

2. $9\frac{1}{8} + 6\frac{2}{4} + 2\frac{10}{16} =$

3. $3\frac{6}{8} + 4\frac{3}{4} =$

4. $7\frac{1}{3} + 5\frac{1}{2} + 6\frac{1}{4} =$

5. $4\frac{4}{9} + 1\frac{1}{2} + 6\frac{2}{3} =$

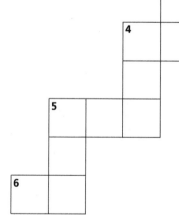

NAME _____ DATE _____

CROSS-NUMBER 5 PUZZLE

SUBTRACTING MIXED FRACTIONS; UNLIKE DENOMINATORS; LOWEST TERMS

Solve the problems below. Remember to express all answers in their lowest terms. Write your answers in the appropriate across and down positions.

 The fraction part of the mixed number should go in its own square.

ACROSS

1. $13 \frac{7}{9} - 1 \frac{1}{3} =$

3. $13 \frac{13}{14} - 6 \frac{4}{7} =$

4. $12 \frac{4}{8} - (4 \frac{3}{4} - 2 \frac{1}{2}) =$

5. $5 \frac{10}{12} - (7 \frac{2}{4} - 4 \frac{1}{3}) =$

6. $9 \frac{5}{6} - 4 \frac{1}{2} =$

DOWN

2. $24 \frac{6}{7} - 1 \frac{1}{2} =$

3. $10 \frac{3}{4} - 3 \frac{8}{16} =$

4. $18 \frac{5}{6} - (1 \frac{1}{2} - 1 \frac{1}{3}) =$

5. $28 \frac{16}{18} - 1 \frac{1}{3} - 1 \frac{2}{9} =$

6. $8 \frac{3}{4} - 3 \frac{1}{3} =$

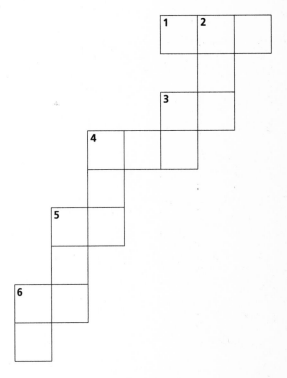

NAME _____ DATE _____

CROSS-NUMBER 6 PUZZLE

MULTIPLYING MIXED FRACTIONS; LOWEST TERMS

Solve the problems below. Remember to express all answers in their lowest terms.

Write your answers in the appropriate across and down positions.

 The fraction part of the mixed number should go in its own square.

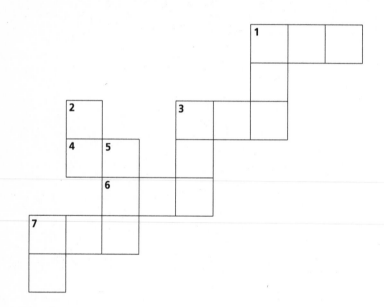

ACROSS

1. $2\frac{1}{2} \times 4\frac{1}{3} =$

3. $4\frac{1}{4} \times 2\frac{2}{3} =$

4. $8 \times 4\frac{1}{4} =$

6. $3\frac{2}{3} \times 7 =$

7. $7\frac{2}{5} \times 3\frac{1}{3} =$

DOWN

1. $4 \times 3\frac{1}{3} =$

2. $3\frac{3}{10} \times 10 =$

3. $5\frac{2}{4} \times 2\frac{2}{3} =$

5. $8 \times 5\frac{1}{3} =$

7. $3\frac{2}{4} \times 6 =$

CROSS-NUMBER
7
PUZZLE

DIVIDING MIXED FRACTIONS; LOWEST TERMS   Solve the problems below. Remember to express all answers in their lowest terms.

Write your answers in the appropriate across and down positions.

 The fraction part of the mixed number should go in its own square.

ACROSS

3. $5 \frac{2}{3} \div \frac{1}{10} =$

4. $2 \frac{5}{3} \div \frac{1}{10} =$

6. $3 \frac{2}{5} \div \frac{1}{8} =$

7. $4 \frac{4}{5} \div \frac{1}{6} =$

8. $2 \frac{1}{3} \div \frac{1}{4} =$

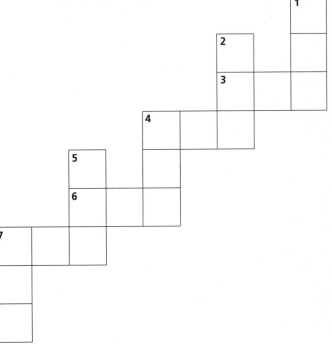

DOWN

1. $4 \frac{2}{3} \div \frac{1}{7} =$

2. $3 \frac{2}{3} \div \frac{1}{7} =$

4. $4 \frac{3}{5} \div \frac{1}{7} =$

5. $3 \frac{1}{5} \div \frac{1}{4} =$

7. $3 \frac{2}{3} \div \frac{1}{8} =$

NAME _____ DATE _____

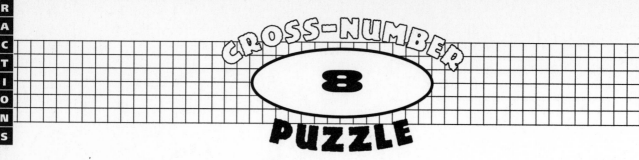

CROSS-NUMBER **8** PUZZLE

ADDING AND SUBTRACTING MIXED FRACTIONS; LOWEST TERMS Solve the problems below. Remember to express all answers in their lowest terms. Write your answers in the appropriate across and down positions.

 The fraction part of the mixed number should go in its own square.

ACROSS

3. $7 \frac{3}{6} + (3 \frac{1}{2} + 10) =$

5. $4 \frac{2}{3} + (9 \frac{3}{4} - 2 \frac{1}{3}) =$

6. $55 \frac{1}{2} - (3 \frac{1}{2} - 2 \frac{2}{4}) =$

7. $14 \frac{8}{9} - 1 \frac{5}{9} =$

8. $7 \frac{2}{12} + 4 \frac{1}{3} + 5 \frac{1}{6} =$

DOWN

1. $5 \frac{1}{2} + 4 \frac{1}{12} + 6 \frac{2}{4} =$

2. $32 \frac{2}{3} - (6 \frac{1}{2} - 5 \frac{1}{3}) =$

4. $16 \frac{2}{3} - 1 \frac{2}{6} =$

7. $7 \frac{1}{3} + 10 \frac{2}{6} =$

9. $4 \frac{2}{4} + (3 \frac{2}{3} - 1 \frac{1}{4}) =$

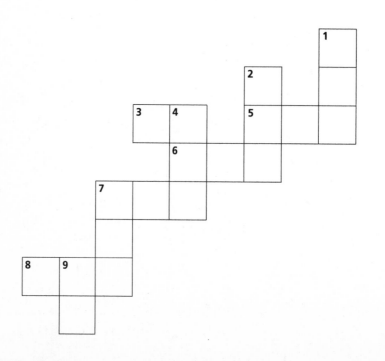

40 CROSS-NUMBER PUZZLES: FRACTIONS, DECIMALS & PERCENTS • SCHOLASTIC TEACHING RESOURCES

CROSS-NUMBER
9
PUZZLE

MULTIPLYING AND DIVIDING MIXED FRACTIONS; LOWEST TERMS   Solve the problems below. Remember to express all answers in their lowest terms. Write your answers in the appropriate across and down positions.

 The fraction part of the mixed number should go in its own square.

ACROSS

1. $1\frac{1}{2} \times 1\frac{1}{6} =$

3. $\frac{2}{4} \div \frac{1}{33} =$

4. $3\frac{2}{3} \div \frac{1}{7} =$

5. $4\frac{4}{5} \times 2\frac{1}{6} =$

6. $2\frac{3}{5} \div \frac{1}{6} =$

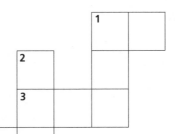

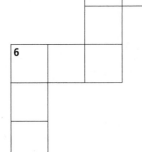

DOWN

1. $2\frac{2}{8} \times 4\frac{2}{3} =$

2. $3\frac{1}{3} \times 6\frac{1}{2} =$

4. $3\frac{2}{5} \div \frac{1}{6} =$

5. $17 \times \frac{4}{5} =$

6. $\frac{4}{6} \div \frac{1}{19} =$

NAME _____ DATE _____

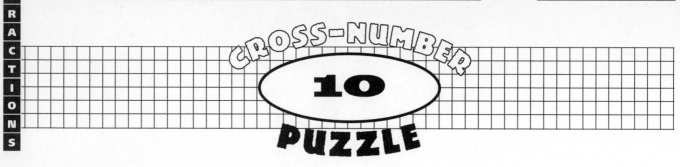

ADDING, SUBTRACTING, MULTIPLYING, AND
DIVIDING MIXED FRACTIONS; LOWEST TERMS

Solve the problems below. Remember to express all
answers in their lowest terms. Write your answers
in the appropriate across and down positions.

The fraction part of the mixed number should go in its own square.

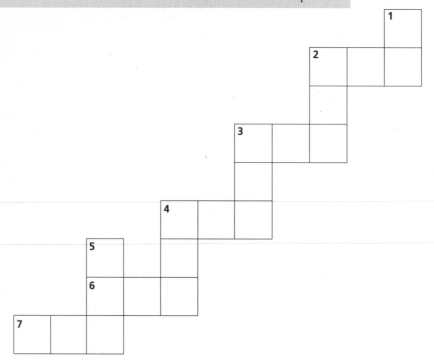

ACROSS

2. $6\frac{3}{4} \times 3\frac{1}{3} =$

3. $4\frac{2}{5} \times 3\frac{3}{4} =$

4. $4\frac{9}{10} + 2\frac{2}{5} + 3\frac{1}{2} =$

6. $12\frac{4}{6} - 2\frac{1}{4} =$

7. $6\frac{2}{8} \times 4\frac{2}{3} =$

DOWN

1. $3\frac{6}{8} \div \frac{5}{6} =$

2. $5\frac{3}{4} + 3\frac{1}{2} + 12\frac{2}{8} =$

3. $3\frac{1}{5} \div \frac{1}{4} =$

4. $6\frac{1}{2} + \frac{2}{3} + 5\frac{1}{4} =$

5. $3\frac{2}{12} + 7\frac{3}{4} + 10\frac{1}{2} =$

40 CROSS-NUMBER PUZZLES: FRACTIONS, DECIMALS & PERCENTS • SCHOLASTIC TEACHING RESOURCES

ADDING; COMMON DENOMINATORS; LOWEST TERMS

Solve the problems below. Remember to express all answers in their lowest terms.

Write your answers in the appropriate across and down positions. The number you record in the outlined box shows where the letter should go in the code boxes at the bottom to solve the riddle.

 The fraction part of the mixed number should go in its own square.

ACROSS

1. $4\frac{2}{5} + \frac{4}{5} + 6\frac{6}{5} =$

3. $\frac{3}{9} + \frac{7}{9} + 3\frac{2}{9} =$

4. $44\frac{6}{9} + 7\frac{5}{9} + 28\frac{6}{9} =$

6. $\frac{6}{5} + \frac{1}{5} + 8\frac{3}{5} + 3\frac{2}{5} =$

7. $3\frac{2}{6} + 14\frac{2}{6} =$

DOWN

1. $73\frac{6}{10} + 73\frac{4}{10} + 7\frac{4}{10} =$

2. $14\frac{2}{16} + 13\frac{14}{16} =$

5. $24\frac{3}{12} + 46\frac{6}{12} + 30\frac{3}{12} =$

6. $8\frac{4}{12} + 3\frac{2}{12} + 5\frac{2}{12} =$

8. $\frac{4}{8} + 7\frac{3}{8} =$

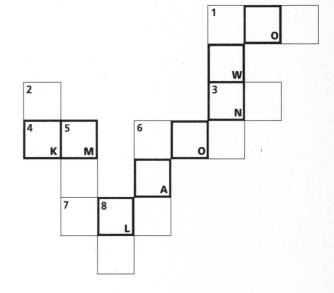

What dance step did the Martian teach the earthlings?

THE

1	2	3	4	5	6	7	8

NAME _____ DATE _____

CROSS-NUMBER 12 PUZZLE

SUBTRACTING; COMMON DENOMINATORS; LOWEST TERMS

Solve the problems below. Remember to express all answers in their lowest terms.

Write your answers in the appropriate across and down positions. The number you record in the outlined box shows where the letter should go in the code boxes at the bottom to solve the riddle.

ACROSS

2. $24 \tfrac{6}{7} - (9 \tfrac{5}{7} - 2 \tfrac{4}{7}) =$

3. $9 \tfrac{9}{12} - 2 \tfrac{2}{12} - 5 \tfrac{1}{12} =$

4. $23 \tfrac{9}{8} - 1 \tfrac{1}{8} - 3 \tfrac{4}{8} =$

6. $16 \tfrac{7}{9} - 3 \tfrac{1}{9} - \tfrac{3}{9} =$

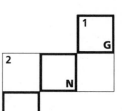

DOWN

1. $20 \tfrac{13}{14} - 12 \tfrac{3}{14} =$

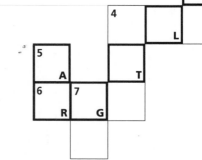

2. $14 \tfrac{5}{8} - (12 \tfrac{7}{8} - 8 \tfrac{6}{8}) =$

3. $26 \tfrac{8}{12} - (3 \tfrac{6}{12} - 1 \tfrac{4}{12}) =$

4. $17 \tfrac{4}{6} - (6 \tfrac{5}{6} - 4 \tfrac{3}{6}) =$

5. $67 \tfrac{7}{10} - 6 \tfrac{7}{10} =$

7. $9 \tfrac{8}{10} - 6 \tfrac{5}{10} =$

Which geometric shape is never wrong?

A | 1 | 2 | 3 | 4 | 5 | | 6 | 7 | 8 | 9 | 0 |

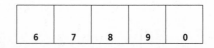

NAME _____ DATE _____

CROSS-NUMBER 13 PUZZLE

MULTIPLYING PROPER FRACTIONS X PROPER FRACTIONS OR WHOLE NUMBERS; LOWEST TERMS

Solve the problems below. Remember to express all answers in their lowest terms. Write your answers in the appropriate across and down positions. The number you record in the outlined box shows where the letter should go in the code boxes at the bottom to solve the riddle.

 The fraction part of the mixed number should go in its own square.

ACROSS

1. $\frac{2}{3} \times \frac{19}{2} =$

2. $21 \times \frac{3}{4} =$

3. $\frac{4}{5} \times 22 =$

5. $\frac{4}{6} \times 19 =$

7. $14 \times \frac{2}{3} =$

DOWN

1. $\frac{3}{4} \times 9 =$

2. $17 \times \frac{4}{5} =$

3. $\frac{2}{3} \times 16 =$

4. $2 \times \frac{41}{2} =$

6. $\frac{34}{3} \times \frac{5}{2} =$

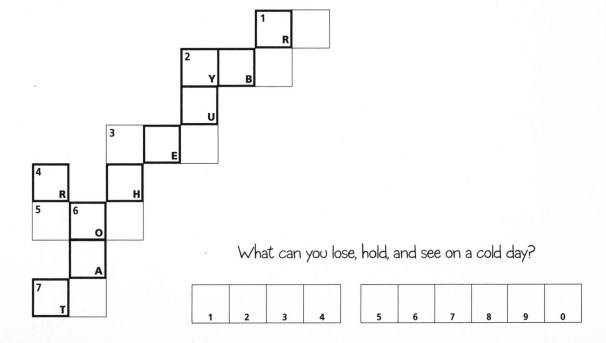

What can you lose, hold, and see on a cold day?

| 1 | 2 | 3 | 4 | | 5 | 6 | 7 | 8 | 9 | 0 |

NAME _____   DATE _____

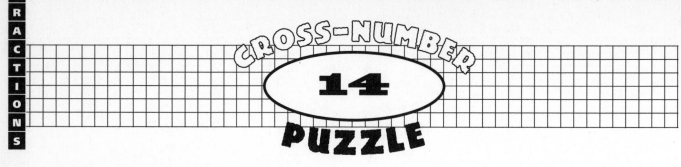

CROSS-NUMBER 14 PUZZLE

DIVIDING PROPER FRACTIONS; LOWEST TERMS   Solve the problems below. Remember to express all answers in their lowest terms. Write your answers in the appropriate across and down positions. The number you record in the outlined box shows where the letter should go in the code boxes at the bottom to solve the riddle.

ACROSS

1. $\frac{1}{2} \div \frac{1}{35} =$

2. $\frac{2}{3} \div \frac{1}{23} =$

3. $\frac{4}{6} \div \frac{1}{35} =$

4. $\frac{3}{4} \div \frac{1}{19} =$

5. $\frac{1}{6} \div \frac{1}{63} =$

DOWN

1. $\frac{1}{6} \div \frac{1}{68} =$

2. $\frac{1}{3} \div \frac{1}{58} =$

3. $\frac{1}{4} \div \frac{1}{113} =$

4. $\frac{2}{4} \div \frac{1}{33} =$

5. $\frac{1}{2} \div \frac{1}{20} =$

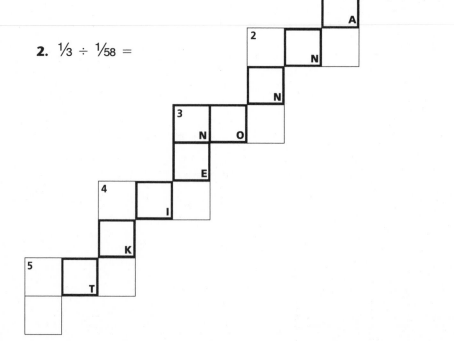

What did the vet prescribe for the pig that had a rash?

1	2		3	4	5	6	7	8	9	0

40 CROSS-NUMBER PUZZLES: FRACTIONS, DECIMALS & PERCENTS © SCHOLASTIC TEACHING RESOURCES

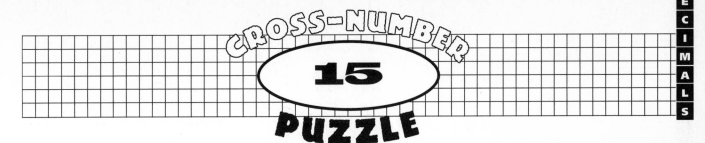

CROSS-NUMBER
15
PUZZLE

| ADDING; 3 ADDENDS | Solve the problems and write your answers in the appropriate across and down positions. |

 The first one has been done for you.

ACROSS

2. 50.48 + 62.43 + 17.83 = *130.74*

4. 953.6 + 72 + 8.46 =

5. 2.8 + 19.63 + 24.09 =

6. 67.03 + .293 + 3.677 =

10. 394.82 + 2.5 + 37.68 =

11. .843 + .067 + .709 =

DOWN

1. 58.76 + 9.4 + 33.847 =

3. 193.4 + 66.2 + 247.9 =

5. 3.334 + .67 + .24 =

7. 7.93 + .776 + 8.42 =

8. 79.42 + .84 + 75.34 =

9. 63.09 + .7 + 24 =

NAME _____   DATE _____

CROSS-NUMBER 16 PUZZLE

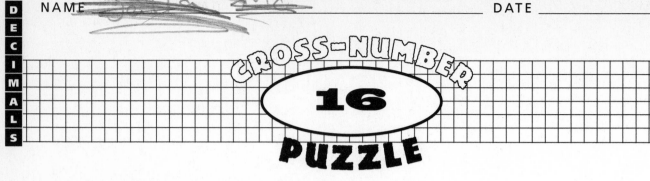

SUBTRACTING; REGROUPING: WHOLE NUMBERS AND TENTHS THROUGH THOUSANDTHS

Solve the following problems and write your answers in the appropriate across and down positions.

ACROSS

1.　4.608
　　− 2.9

3.　34.16
　　− 10.93

5.　6.007
　　− 2.039

7.　56.347
　　− 42.902

8.　9.156
　　− 4.38

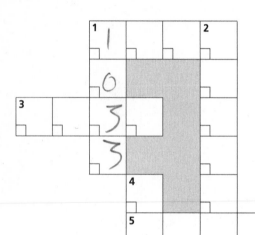
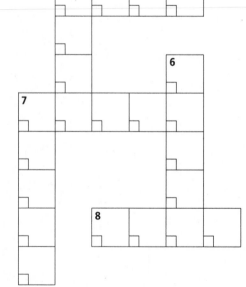

DOWN

1.　72.3
　　− 62.03
　　10.33

2.　843.6
　　− 2.924

4.　28
　　− 4.667

6.　43.007
　　− 17.3

7.　17
　　− 1.835

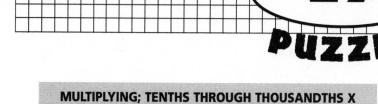

CROSS-NUMBER 17 PUZZLE

MULTIPLYING; TENTHS THROUGH THOUSANDTHS X WHOLE NUMBERS, TENTHS, OR HUNDREDTHS

Solve the problems and write your answers in the appropriate across and down positions.

ACROSS

3.
$$\begin{array}{r} .947 \\ \times\ \ 6.7 \end{array}$$

4.
$$\begin{array}{r} 600 \\ \times\ \ .92 \end{array}$$

5.
$$\begin{array}{r} 3.91 \\ \times\ \ .36 \end{array}$$

7.
$$\begin{array}{r} 9.36 \\ \times\ \ 4.6 \end{array}$$

9.
$$\begin{array}{r} .080 \\ \times\ \ .85 \end{array}$$

DOWN

1.
$$\begin{array}{r} 7.19 \\ \times\ \ 3.8 \end{array}$$

2.
$$\begin{array}{r} 83.9 \\ \times\ \ 2.8 \end{array}$$

4.
$$\begin{array}{r} 74.8 \\ \times\ \ 75 \end{array}$$

6.
$$\begin{array}{r} .006 \\ \times\ \ 2.5 \end{array}$$

8.
$$\begin{array}{r} .583 \\ \times\ \ 67 \end{array}$$

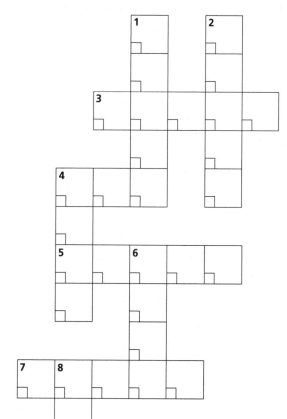

D
E
C
I
M
A
L
S

CROSS-NUMBER 18 PUZZLE

DIVIDING; 2-DIGIT DECIMAL DIVISOR

Solve the problems and write your answers in the appropriate across and down positions.

ACROSS

2. $.29 \overline{)127.60}$

4. $.32 \overline{)17.184}$

5. $.71 \overline{)5.9143}$

6. $.93 \overline{)9.0303}$

7. $.66 \overline{)1.9272}$

8. $4.7 \overline{)28.435}$

DOWN

1. $5.9 \overline{)22.184}$

2. $6.3 \overline{)30.177}$

3. $3.8 \overline{)3.4808}$

4. $.59 \overline{)31.506}$

5. $.61 \overline{)50.203}$

7. $.23 \overline{)5.865}$

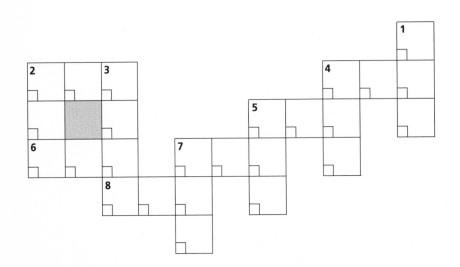

48 CROSS-NUMBER PUZZLES: FRACTIONS, DECIMALS & PERCENTS • SCHOLASTIC TEACHING RESOURCES

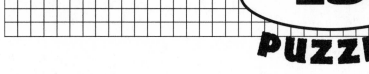

CROSS-NUMBER
19
PUZZLE

| ADDING; 3 ADDENDS | Solve the problems and write your answers in the across and down positions. The number you record in the outlined box shows where the letter should go in the code boxes at the bottom to solve the riddle. |

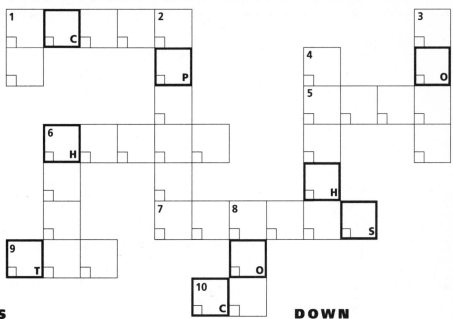

ACROSS

1. 39.37
  842.06
  + 71.50

5. 29.06
  .68
  + 4.34

6. 3.706
  92
  + 6.534

7. 923.71
  .8
  + 4.634

9. 44.3
  649.7
  + 86

10. 64.6
  7.4
  + 8

DOWN

1. .593
  8.83
  + .377

2. 247.07
  6.77
  + 84.369

3. .397
  .246
  + .039

4. 9.62
  13.474
  + .5

6. 4.67
  7.93
  + 5.98

8. 837.4
  58.5
  + 24.1

What game do kangaroos like to play at recess?

1	2	3	4	5	6	7	8	9

DECIMALS

CROSS-NUMBER 20 PUZZLE

SUBTRACTING; REGROUPING: WHOLE NUMBERS
AND TENTHS THROUGH THOUSANDTHS

Solve the problems and write your answers in the across and down positions. The number you record in the outlined box shows where the letter should go in the code boxes at the bottom to solve the riddle.

ACROSS

1.
    57.61
  − 48.07
  _____
  11.66

4.
    59.01
  − 6.40

6.
   862.391
  − 47.555

8.
   392.11
  − 47.09

10.
    4.307
  − 3.1

DOWN

2.
    76.344
  − 34.726

3.
   267.841
  − 79.009

5.
     6.339
  − 2.176

7.
   184.37
  − 49.66

9.
   647.82
  − 73.09

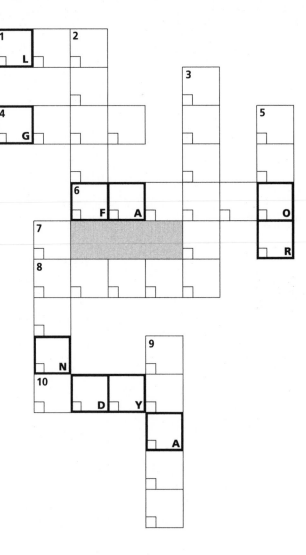

What fire-breathing insect was never slain by a knight?

1	2	3	4	5	6	7	8	9	0

40 CROSS-NUMBER PUZZLES: FRACTIONS, DECIMALS & PERCENTS • SCHOLASTIC TEACHING RESOURCES

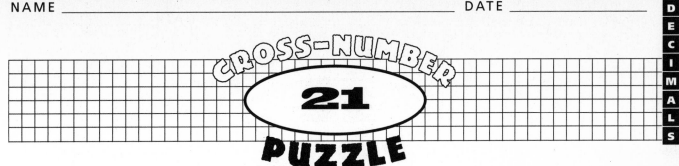

CROSS-NUMBER
21
PUZZLE

| **MULTIPLYING; TENTHS THROUGH THOUSANDTHS X WHOLE NUMBERS** |

Solve the problems and write your answers in the across and down positions. The number you record in the outlined box shows where the letter should go in the code boxes at the bottom to solve the riddle.

ACROSS

1.   50.6
× 4.8

3.   9.77
× 43

5.   .940
× 67

7.   67.2
× 89

8.   619
× 7.6

10.   .846
× 64

DOWN

1.   7.94
× 36

2.   3.28
× 63

4.   4.93
× 28

6.   .735
× 39

7.   823
× 6.7

9.   578
× 8.5

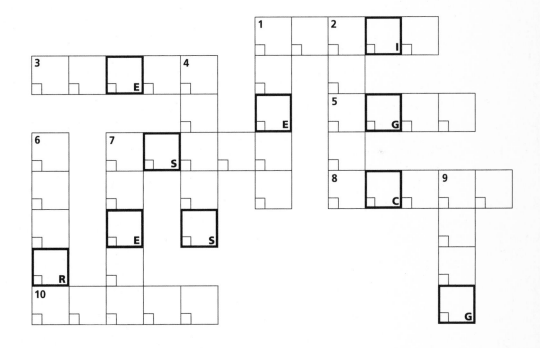

Why did the chicken sprint around the barnyard four times a day?

| | | | | — | | | | | |
|1|2|3|4| |5|6|7|8|9|0|

NAME _____ DATE _____

CROSS-NUMBER 22 PUZZLE

DIVIDING; 1-DIGIT WHOLE NUMBER DIVISOR Solve the problems and write your answers in the across and down positions. The number you record in the outlined box shows where the letter should go in the code boxes at the bottom to solve the riddle.

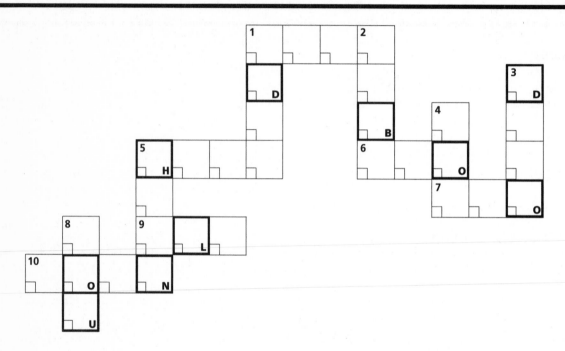

ACROSS

1. $4 \overline{)\ 30.536}$

5. $7 \overline{)\ 4,504.5}$

6. $9 \overline{)\ 339.3}$

7. $5 \overline{)\ 47.15}$

9. $8 \overline{)\ 58.24}$

10. $3 \overline{)\ 2,543.7}$

DOWN

1. $9 \overline{)\ 6,331.5}$

2. $5 \overline{)\ 24.565}$

3. $7 \overline{)\ 403.41}$

4. $7 \overline{)\ 19.53}$

5. $4 \overline{)\ 2,551.6}$

8. $6 \overline{)\ 568.8}$

What kind of dog would Count Dracula want as a pet?

1	2	3	4	5	6	7	8	9	0

| ADDING; 3 ADDENDS | Express each problem in its numerical form. Then solve the problems and write your answers in the appropriate across and down positions. |

 The word "and" separates the whole number from the decimal.

ACROSS

1. Add the following numbers: forty-eight and sixty-three hundredths; three and fifty-seven hundredths; twenty-six and eight tenths.

3. Add the following numbers: fifty-nine and thirty-one hundredths; four and seventy-five hundredths; six and eight tenths.

5. Add the following numbers: fifty-eight and six tenths; seven and ninety-three hundredths; six and forty-seven hundredths.

6. Add the following numbers: forty-nine and seventy-eight hundredths; thirty-four hundredths; six and nine hundredths.

7. Add the following numbers: eight and three hundred three thousandths; seventy-nine hundredths; two and five tenths.

DOWN

2. Add the following numbers: nine hundred forty-seven and six tenths; twenty-four and thirty-six hundredths; five and six tenths.

4. Add the following numbers: thirty-nine and six hundredths; twenty-four; four and four hundredths.

6. Add the following numbers: fifty and nine hundredths; four and one hundredth; three and ninety-one hundredths.

7. Add the following numbers: six and forty-three hundredths; six hundred sixty-seven thousandths; four and one tenth.

8. Add the following numbers: eighteen and forty-eight hundredths; seven and fifty-nine hundredths; ten and fourteen hundredths.

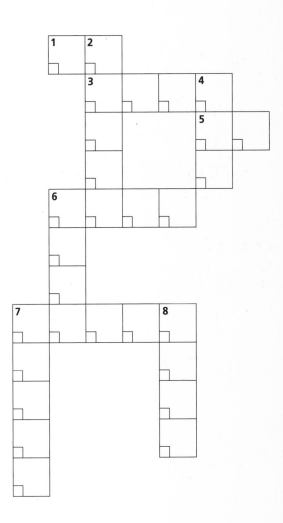

DECIMALS

CROSS-NUMBER

24

PUZZLE

SUBTRACTING; REGROUPING; WHOLE NUMBERS AND TENTHS THROUGH THOUSANDTHS

Express each problem in its numerical form. Then solve the problems and write your answers in the appropriate across and down positions.

 The word "and" separates the whole number from the decimal.

ACROSS

2. Subtract thirty-nine and forty-two hundredths from forty-three and thirty-four hundredths.

3. Subtract sixty-one and seventy-eight hundredths from nine hundred three and seventy-two hundredths.

7. Subtract thirty-two and sixty-two hundredths from three hundred sixty-four and five tenths.

9. Subtract four and seven hundred twenty-two thousandths from six and ninety-three hundredths.

10. Subtract eight and seven thousandths from sixty-two and five hundredths.

DOWN

1. Subtract twenty and four hundred fifteen thousandths from twenty-four and three hundred twenty-three thousandths.

4. Subtract two and eight hundred thirty-seven thousandths from one hundred sixty-seven and four tenths.

5. Subtract two and nine hundred thirty-eight thousandths from seven and one hundred sixty-five thousandths.

6. Subtract three and one hundred fifty-two thousandths from twenty-three and twenty-one hundredths.

8. Subtract six and ninety-seven hundredths from forty-three and nine thousandths.

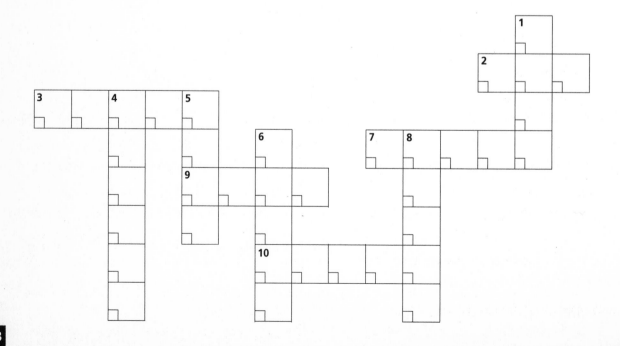

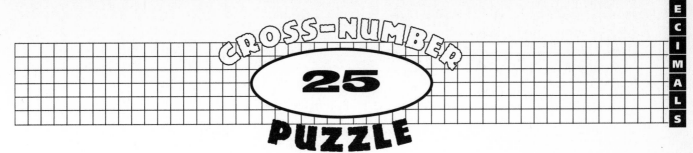

CROSS-NUMBER
25
PUZZLE

| MULTIPLYING; TENTHS AND HUNDREDTHS X TENTHS | Express each multiplication problem in its numerical form. Then solve the |

problems and write your answers as a decimal in the appropriate across and down positions.

 The word "and" separates the whole number from the decimal.

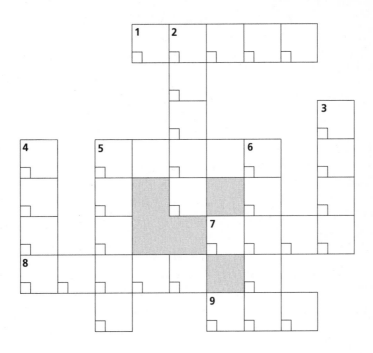

ACROSS

1. Multiply ninety-six and eight tenths by eight and six tenths.

5. Multiply seven and eighty-two hundredths by six and seven tenths.

7. Multiply eight and twenty-four hundredths by seven tenths.

8. Multiply seven and seventy-three hundredths by six and eight tenths.

9. Multiply sixty-four by eight tenths.

DOWN

2. Multiply forty-three and nine tenths by eight and eight tenths.

3. Multiply twenty-five and seven tenths by three and four tenths.

4. Multiply five and eighty-five hundredths by nine tenths.

5. Multiply sixty-four and nine tenths by nine and one tenth.

6. Multiply eight and nine hundredths by five and nine tenths.

CROSS-NUMBER 26 PUZZLE

DIVIDING; 2-DIGIT WHOLE NUMBER DIVISOR

Express each division problem in its numerical form. Then solve the problems and write your answers as a decimal in the appropriate across and down positions.

 The word "and" separates the whole number from the decimal.

ACROSS

2. Divide forty-four thousand nine hundred forty-three and six tenths by fifty-two.

4. Divide two thousand seven hundred fifty-five and seventy-two hundredths by forty-four.

6. Divide four hundred ninety-four and ninety-four hundredths by seventy-three.

8. Divide five thousand one hundred eight and four tenths by eighty-six.

10. Divide four hundred sixty-one and forty-eight hundredths by eighty-three.

DOWN

1. Divide seven thousand two hundred ninety-five and six tenths by ninety-two.

3. Divide three hundred nine and seven hundred twenty-nine thousandths by forty-nine.

5. Divide twenty-two thousand two hundred seven and six tenths by fifty-nine.

7. Divide six thousand two hundred forty-seven and two hundredths by seventy-eight.

9. Divide three hundred fifty and three hundred sixteen thousandths by thirty-seven.

40 CROSS-NUMBER PUZZLES: FRACTIONS, DECIMALS & PERCENTS • SCHOLASTIC TEACHING RESOURCES

CROSS-NUMBER **27** PUZZLE

50% OF 60 IS N.	Solve the problems and express each answer as a decimal. Write your answers in the appropriate across and down positions.

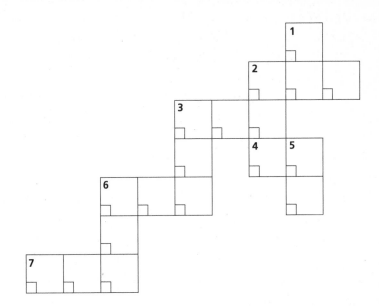

ACROSS

2. 51% of 60 =

3. 51% of 70 =

4. 90% of 60 =

6. 85% of 90 =

7. 44% of 110 =

DOWN

1. 50% of 60 =

2. 15% of 25 =

3. 55% of 70 =

5. 80% of 60 =

6. 56% of 140 =

CROSS-NUMBER 28 PUZZLE

| 100 IS 20% OF N. | Solve the problems and express each answer as a whole number. Write your answers in the appropriate across and down positions. |

ACROSS

3. 81 is 75% of _____ .

5. 60 is 6% of _____ .

6. 902 is 44% of _____ .

7. 60 is 30% of _____ .

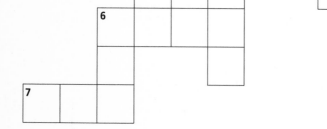

DOWN

1. 35 is 25% of _____ .

2. 30 is 4% of _____ .

3. 350 is 25% of _____ .

4. 24 is 8% of _____ .

5. 110 is 10% of _____ .

6. 243 is 90% of _____ .

CROSS-NUMBER 29 PUZZLE

| 10 IS N% OF 100. | Solve the problems and express each answer as a whole number. Complete the puzzle by spelling out your answers in the appropriate across and down positions. |

ACROSS

1. 14 is _____% of 20.

3. 132 is _____% of 200.

5. 7 is _____% of 14.

7. 12 is _____% of 30.

9. 18 is _____% of 20.

10. 5 is _____% of 20.

DOWN

1. 18 is _____% of 30.

2. 66 is _____% of 200.

4. 12 is _____% of 60.

5. 8 is _____% of 16.

6. 6 is _____% of 30.

8. 9 is _____% of 90.

PERCENTS

CROSS-NUMBER
30
PUZZLE

CALCULATING DISCOUNTS   What percent of the original price is the new discount? Calculate this percent. Spell out your answers in the appropriate across and down positions.

ACROSS

	ORIGINAL PRICE	DISCOUNT	PERCENT DISCOUNT
4.	$200	$32	_____ %
6.	$15	$12	_____ %
7.	$75	$7.50	_____ %
8.	$500	$250	_____ %
10.	$150	$60	_____ %
11.	$150	$30	_____ %

DOWN

	ORIGINAL PRICE	DISCOUNT	PERCENT DISCOUNT
1.	$200	$10	_____ %
2.	$200	$120	_____ %
3.	$240	$60	_____ %
5.	$110	$8.80	_____ %
9.	$45	$6.75	_____ %
12.	$50	$5	_____ %

CROSS-NUMBER 31 PUZZLE

12 IS N% OF 60.

Solve the problems and express each answer as a whole number. Complete the puzzle by spelling out your answers in the appropriate across and down positions. The number in the outlined box shows where the letter should go in the code boxes at the bottom to solve this riddle.

ACROSS

1. 18 is _____ % of 24.

4. 20 is _____ % of 25.

7. 9 is _____ % of 10.

8. 42 is _____ % of 105.

9. 18 is _____ % of 120.

DOWN

1. 36 is _____ % of 60.

2. 24 is _____ % of 48.

3. 24 is _____ % of 32.

5. 10 is _____ % of 40.

6. 36 is _____ % of 72.

What did the shepherd shout to the female sheep?

1 2 3   4 5 6

NAME _____ DATE _____

CROSS-NUMBER 32 PUZZLE

N% OF 72 IS 36. Solve the problems and express each answer as a whole number. Complete the puzzle by spelling out your answers in the appropriate across and down positions. The number in the outlined box shows where the letter should go in the code boxes at the bottom to solve this riddle.

ACROSS

3. _____% of 60 is 36.

6. _____% of 50 is 49.

7. _____% of 300 is 108.

8. _____% of 80 is 60.

10. _____% of 1,000 is 810.

DOWN

1. _____% of 100 is 60.

2. _____% of 38 is 19.

4. _____% of 60 is 12.

5. _____% of 400 is 352.

9. _____% of 250 is 5.

What can a penguin get if it sits on the ice too long?

1	2	3	4	5	B	6	7	8

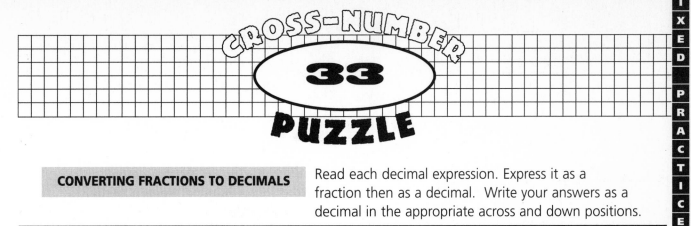

CONVERTING FRACTIONS TO DECIMALS   Read each decimal expression. Express it as a fraction then as a decimal. Write your answers as a decimal in the appropriate across and down positions.

ACROSS

3. five and eight tenths   _____ _____

4. twenty-seven and fifteen hundredths   _____ _____

5. eleven and one hundred twenty-one thousandths   _____ _____

7. twenty-six and thirteen thousandths   _____ _____

9. three and three thousandths   _____ _____

10. seven and seven hundred three thousandths   _____ _____

DOWN

1. six and eighty-two hundredths   _____ _____

2. sixteen and one hundred one thousandths   _____ _____

5. thirteen and seven hundredths   _____ _____

6. fourteen and three hundredths   _____ _____

7. twenty-one and seven tenths   _____ _____

8. three and thirty-three thousandths   _____ _____

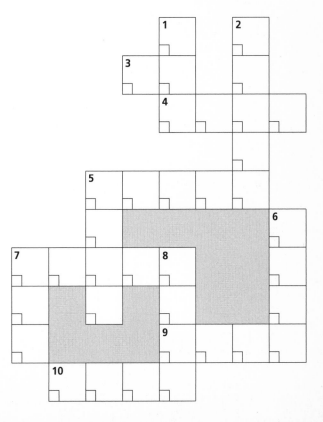

MIXED PRACTICE

CROSS-NUMBER
34
PUZZLE

| CONVERTING FRACTIONS TO DECIMALS | Solve each problem and express the answer as a decimal. Write your answers in the appropriate across and down positions. |

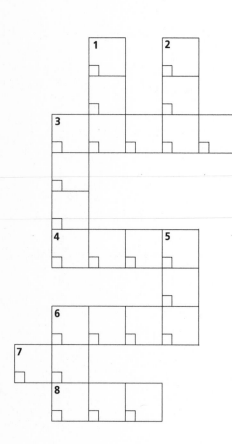

ACROSS

3. $4 \frac{3}{10} + 2 \frac{3}{100} + 5 \frac{3}{1000} =$

4. $3 \frac{2}{8} + 4 \frac{187}{1000} =$

6. $4 \frac{2}{4} + 7 \frac{2}{5} + 5 \frac{3}{100} =$

7. $9 \frac{8}{10} - 3 \frac{1}{5} - 2 \frac{1}{2} =$

8. $4 \frac{15}{20} - 1 \frac{14}{100} =$

DOWN

1. $7 \frac{51}{100} - 2 \frac{5}{10} =$

2. $13 \frac{21}{25} - 5 \frac{14}{20} - 2 \frac{1}{100} =$

3. $5 \frac{3}{5} + 1 \frac{2}{10} + 5 \frac{7}{100} =$

5. $5 \frac{83}{100} - \frac{7}{10} + 2 \frac{3}{5} =$

6. $7 \frac{7}{10} - 4 \frac{9}{20} - 2 \frac{3}{25} =$

NAME _____ DATE _____

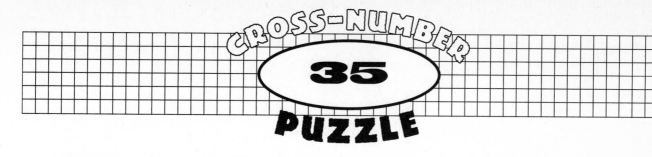

CONVERTING DECIMALS TO PERCENTS Express each decimal as a percent. Write your answers in the appropriate across and down positions.

ACROSS

2. .66 = _____%

3. 2.4 = _____%

4. 1.2 = _____%

5. 7.5 = _____%

6. .35 = _____%

DOWN

1. .36 = _____%

2. 6.5 = _____%

3. 2.2 = _____%

4. 1.35 = _____%

5. .75 = _____%

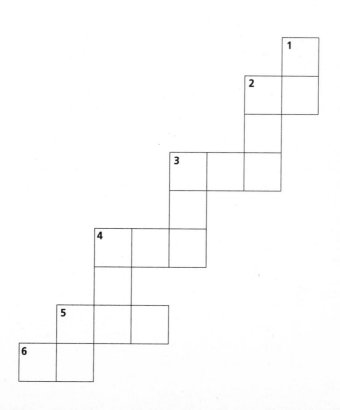

MIXED PRACTICE

CONVERTING FRACTIONS TO PERCENTS

Express each fraction as a percent. Write your answers in the appropriate across and down positions.

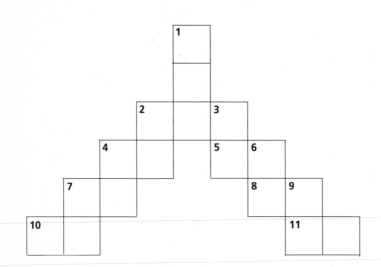

ACROSS

2. $^{52}/_{50}$ = _____%

4. $^{13}/_{20}$ = _____%

5. $^{174}/_{200}$ = _____%

7. $^{18}/_{25}$ = _____%

8. $^{52}/_{100}$ = _____%

10. $^{7}/_{20}$ = _____%

11. $^{30}/_{75}$ = _____%

DOWN

1. $^{6}/_{6}$ = _____%

2. $^{18}/_{120}$ = _____%

3. $^{12}/_{25}$ = _____%

4. $^{31}/_{50}$ = _____%

6. $^{24}/_{32}$ = _____%

7. $^{30}/_{40}$ = _____%

9. $^{6}/_{25}$ = _____%

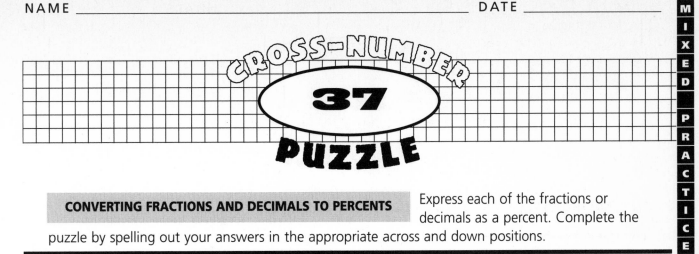

CONVERTING FRACTIONS AND DECIMALS TO PERCENTS Express each of the fractions or decimals as a percent. Complete the puzzle by spelling out your answers in the appropriate across and down positions.

ACROSS

2. .5 = _____%

4. ⁴⁄₅ = _____%

6. ³⁵⁄₅₀ = _____%

7. .08 = _____%

9. ¹³⁄₂₀ = _____%

DOWN

1. ¹⁸⁄₂₅ = _____%

2. .15 = _____%

3. ²³⁄₅₀ = _____%

5. .9 = _____%

8. ⁴⁄₂₅ = _____%

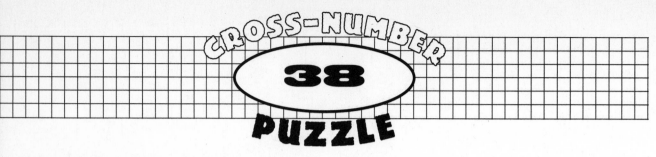

CROSS-NUMBER 38 PUZZLE

CONVERTING PERCENTS TO FRACTIONS; LOWEST TERMS

Express the following percents as fractions in the simplest form.

Complete the puzzle by spelling out the numerators in the appropriate across and down positions.

ACROSS

1. 32% =

4. 72% =

5. 40% =

7. 90% =

8. 20% =

DOWN

1. 55% =

2. 70% =

3. 30% =

5. 48% =

6. 25% =

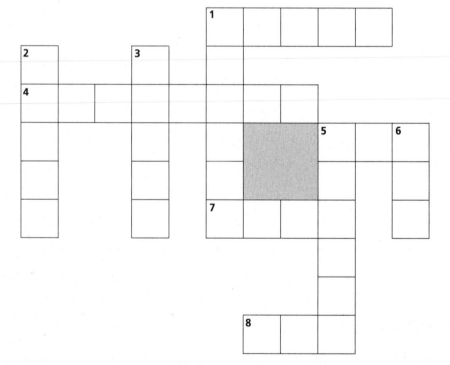

CROSS-NUMBER 39 PUZZLE

MIXED OPERATIONS Solve each problem by starting with the first number and working from left to right. Write your answers in the appropriate across and down positions.

ACROSS

3. 26.16   ➧ Divide by .6   ➧ Subtract 4.9   ➧ Add 30.04   = _____

5. 48.2   ➧ Multiply by 2.7   ➧ Subtract 115.5   ➧ Add .243   = _____

7. 7.5   ➧ Add 5.08   ➧ Divide by .2   ➧ Subtract 3.4   = _____

8. 5.139   ➧ Divide by .9   ➧ Add 4.09   ➧ Multiply by 7.13   = _____

9. 97.63   ➧ Subtract 43.072   ➧ Add 41   ➧ Multiply by 3   = _____

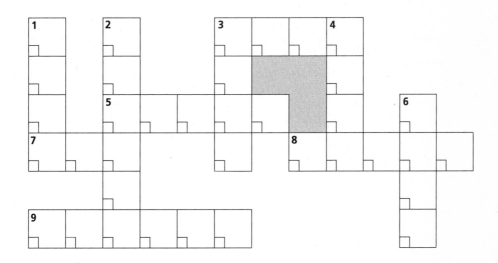

DOWN

1. 9.23   ➧ Multiply by 3.3   ➧ Add 5.011   ➧ Subtract 15.02   = _____

2. 6.34   ➧ Add 17.007   ➧ Multiply by 8   ➧ Subtract 5.2   = _____

3. 55.55   ➧ Add 14.37   ➧ Subtract 60.8   ➧ Multiply by .7   = _____

4. 58.4   ➧ Subtract 23.72   ➧ Add 15.9   ➧ Subtract 2.39   = _____

6. 25.1   ➧ Multiply by 3.9   ➧ Add 8.65   ➧ Subtract 9.33   = _____

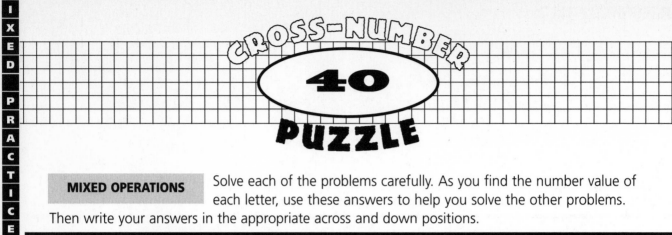

CROSS-NUMBER
40
PUZZLE

MIXED OPERATIONS   Solve each of the problems carefully. As you find the number value of each letter, use these answers to help you solve the other problems. Then write your answers in the appropriate across and down positions.

 Finish the problems that give you numbers to work with first.

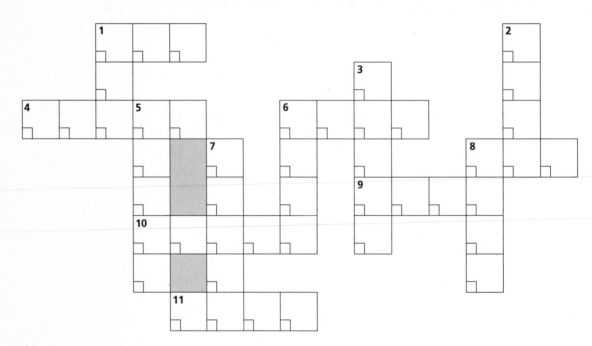

ACROSS

1. $N = C \times 6 - R =$

4. $R = M - C =$

6. $C = 5.8 + 7.03 - 6.426 =$

8. $X = 12.6 + 15.3 - 1.4 =$

9. $Z = (R + X) - P =$

10. $V = P \times 6 =$

11. $P = 29.92 \div .8 + 4.24 =$

DOWN

1. $F = 3.6 \div 12 \times 51 =$

2. $D = E - M + 3.1 =$

3. $E = A + C =$

5. $M = 59.74 - 33.012 =$

6. $T = E - (5.0 \times 4.8) =$

7. $Y = V - 20.03 =$

8. $A = 3.7 \times 6.5 =$

ANSWER KEY

Puzzle #1
ACROSS
1. 7; seven
4. 5; five
5. 6; six
7. 50; fifty
9. 14; fourteen
11. 19; nineteen
DOWN
2. 8; eight
3. 6; six
4. 15; fifteen
6. 11; eleven
8. 4; four
10. 10; ten

Puzzle #2
ACROSS
1. 21; twenty-one
3. 40; forty
5. 9; nine
6. 8; eight
8. 20; twenty
10. 16; sixteen
DOWN
1. 36; thirty-six
2. 18; eighteen
3. 15; fifteen
4. 10; ten
7. 12; twelve
9. 30; thirty

Puzzle #3
ACROSS
4. 8; eight
6. 3; three
7. 7; seven
9. 9; nine
10. 4; four
11. 9; nine
DOWN
1. 4; four
2. 7; seven
3. 5; five
5. 2; two
6. 3; three
7. 7; seven

Puzzle #4
ACROSS
2. 11 7/9
3. 8 1/4
4. 1 1/2
5. 11 1/12
6. 2 11/18
DOWN
1. 12 7/9
2. 18 1/4
3. 8 1/2
4. 19 1/12
5. 12 11/18

Puzzle #5
ACROSS
1. 12 4/9
3. 7 5/14
4. 10 1/4
5. 2 2/3
6. 5 1/3
DOWN
2. 23 5/14
3. 7 1/4
4. 18 2/3
5. 26 1/3
6. 5 5/12

Puzzle #6
ACROSS
1. 10 5/6
3. 11 1/3
4. 34
6. 25 2/3
7. 24 2/3
DOWN
1. 13 1/3
2. 33
3. 14 2/3
5. 42 2/3
7. 21

Puzzle #7
ACROSS
3. 56 2/3
4. 36 2/3
6. 27 1/5
7. 28 4/5
8. 9 1/3
DOWN
1. 32 2/3
2. 25 2/3
4. 32 1/5
5. 12 4/5
7. 29 1/3

Puzzle #8
ACROSS
3. 21
5. 12 1/12
6. 54 1/2
7. 13 1/3
8. 16 2/3
DOWN
1. 16 1/12
2. 31 1/2
4. 15 1/3
7. 17 2/3
9. 6 11/12

Puzzle #9
ACROSS
1. 1 3/4
3. 16 1/2
4. 25 2/3
5. 10 2/5
6. 15 3/5
DOWN
1. 10 1/2
2. 21 2/3
4. 20 2/5
5. 13 3/5
6. 12 2/3

Puzzle #10
ACROSS
2. 22 1/2
3. 16 1/2
4. 10 4/5
6. 10 5/12
7. 29 1/6
DOWN
1. 4 1/2
2. 21 1/2
3. 12 4/5
4. 12 5/12
5. 21 1/6

Puzzle #11
ACROSS
1. 12 2/5
3. 4 1/3
4. 81
6. 13 2/5
7. 17 2/3
DOWN
1. 154 2/5
2. 28
5. 101
6. 16 2/3
8. 7 7/8
What dance step did the Martian teach the earthlings?
THE MOONWALK

Puzzle #12
ACROSS
2. 17 5/7
3. 2 1/2
4. 19 1/2
6. 13 1/3
DOWN
1. 8 5/7
2. 10 1/2
3. 24 1/2
4. 15 1/3
5. 61
7. 3 3/10
Which geometric shape is never wrong?
A RIGHT ANGLE

Puzzle #13

ACROSS
1. 6 1/3
2. 15 3/4
3. 17 3/5
5. 12 2/3
7. 9 1/3

DOWN
1. 6 3/4
2. 13 3/5
3. 10 2/3
4. 41
6. 28 1/3

What can you lose, hold, and see on a cold day?
YOUR BREATH

Puzzle #14

ACROSS
1. 17 1/2
2. 15 1/3
3. 23 1/3
4. 14 1/4
5. 10 1/2

DOWN
1. 11 1/3
2. 19 1/3
3. 28 1/4
4. 16 1/2
5. 10

What did the vet prescribe for the pig that had a rash?
AN OINKMENT

Puzzle #15

ACROSS
2. 130.74
4. 1034.06
5. 46.52
6. 71
10. 435
11. 1.619

DOWN
1. 102.007
3. 507.5
5. 4.244
7. 17.126
8. 155.6
9. 87.79

Puzzle #16

ACROSS
1. 1.708
3. 23.23
5. 3.968
7. 13.445
8. 4.776

DOWN
1. 10.27
2. 840.626
4. 23.333
6. 25.707
7. 15.165

Puzzle #17

ACROSS
3. 6.3449
4. 552
5. 1.4076
7. 43.056
9. 0.068

DOWN
1. 27.322
2. 234.92
4. 5610
6. 0.015
8. 39.061

Puzzle #18

ACROSS
2. 440
4. 53.7
5. 8.33
6. 9.71
7. 2.92
8. 6.05

DOWN
1. 3.76
2. 4.79
3. 0.916
4. 53.4
5. 82.3
7. 25.5

Puzzle #19

ACROSS
1. 952.93
5. 34.08
6. 102.24
7. 929.144
9. 780
10. 80

DOWN
1. 9.8
2. 338.209
3. 0.682
4. 23.594
6. 18.58
8. 920

What game do kangaroos like to play at recess?
HOPSCOTCH

Puzzle #20

ACROSS
1. 9.54
4. 52.61
6. 814.836
8. 345.02
10. 1.207

DOWN
2. 41.618
3. 188.832
5. 4.163
7. 134.71
9. 574.73

What fire-breathing insect was never slain by a knight?
A DRAGONFLY

Puzzle #21

ACROSS
1. 242.88
3. 420.11
5. 62.98
7. 5,980.8
8. 4,704.4
10. 54.144

DOWN
1. 285.84
2. 206.64
4. 138.04
6. 28.665
7. 5,514.1
9. 4,913

Why did the chicken sprint around the barnyard four times a day?
EGGS-ERCISE

Puzzle #22

ACROSS
1. 7.634
5. 643.5
6. 37.7
7. 9.43
9. 7.28
10. 847.9

DOWN
1. 703.5
2. 4.913
3. 57.63
4. 2.79
5. 637.9
8. 94.8

What kind of dog would Count Dracula want as a pet?
BLOODHOUND

Puzzle #23
ACROSS
1. 79
3. 70.86
5. 73
6. 56.21
7. 11.593
DOWN
2. 977.56
4. 67.1
6. 58.01
7. 11.197
8. 36.21

Puzzle #24
ACROSS
2. 3.92
3. 841.94
7. 331.88
9. 2.208
10. 54.043
DOWN
1. 3.908
4. 164.563
5. 4.227
6. 20.058
8. 36.039

Puzzle #25
ACROSS
1. 832.48
5. 52.394
7. 5.768
8. 52.564
9. 51.2
DOWN
2. 386.32
3. 87.38
4. 5.265
5. 590.59
6. 47.731

Puzzle #26
ACROSS
2. 864.3
4. 62.63
6. 6.78
8. 59.4
10. 5.56

DOWN
1. 79.3
3. 6.321
5. 376.4
7. 80.09
9. 9.468

Puzzle #27
ACROSS
2. 30.6
3. 35.7
4. 54
6. 76.5
7. 48.4
DOWN
1. 30
2. 3.75
3. 38.5
5. 48
6. 78.4

Puzzle #28
ACROSS
3. 108
5. 1,000
6. 2,050
7. 200
DOWN
1. 140
2. 750
3. 1,400
4. 300
5. 1,100
6. 270

Puzzle #29
ACROSS
1. 70; seventy
3. 66; sixty-six
5. 50; fifty
7. 40; forty
9. 90; ninety
10. 25; twenty-five
DOWN
1. 60; sixty
2. 33; thirty-three
4. 20; twenty
5. 50; fifty
6. 20; twenty
8. 10; ten

Puzzle #30
ACROSS
4. 16; sixteen
6. 80; eighty
7. 10; ten
8. 50; fifty
10. 40; forty
11. 20; twenty
DOWN
1. 5; five
2. 60; sixty
3. 25; twenty-five
5. 8; eight
9. 15; fifteen
12. 10; ten

Puzzle #31
ACROSS
1. 75; seventy-five
4. 80; eighty
7. 90; ninety
8. 40; forty
9. 15; fifteen
DOWN
1. 60; sixty
2. 50; fifty
3. 75; seventy-five
5. 25; twenty-five
6. 50; fifty
*What did the shepherd
shout to the female
sheep?*
HEY EWE

Puzzle #32
ACROSS
3. 60; sixty
6. 98; ninety-eight
7. 36; thirty-six
8. 75; seventy-five
10. 81; eighty-one
DOWN
1. 60; sixty
2. 50; fifty
4. 20; twenty
5. 88; eighty-eight
9. 2; two
*What can a penguin
get if it sits on the ice
too long?*
FROSTBITE

Puzzle #33
ACROSS
3. 5.8
4. 27.15
5. 11.121
7. 26.013
9. 3.003
10. 7.703
DOWN
1. 6.82
2. 16.101
5. 13.07
6. 14.03
7. 21.7
8. 3.033

Puzzle #34
ACROSS
3. 11.333
4. 7.437
6. 16.93
7. 4.1
8. 3.61
DOWN
1. 5.01
2. 6.13
3. 11.87
5. 7.73
6. 1.13

Puzzle #35
ACROSS
2. 66
3. 240
4. 120
5. 750
6. 35
DOWN
1. 36
2. 650
3. 220
4. 135
5. 75

Puzzle #36
ACROSS
  2. 104
  4. 65
  5. 87
  7. 72
  8. 52
10. 35
11. 40
DOWN
  1. 100
  2. 15
  3. 48
  4. 62
  6. 75
  7. 75
  9. 24

Puzzle #37
ACROSS
  2. 50; fifty
  4. 80; eighty
  6. 70; seventy
  7. 8; eight
  9. 65; sixty-five
DOWN
  1. 72; seventy-two
  2. 15; fifteen
  3. 46; forty-six
  5. 90; ninety
  8. 16; sixteen

Puzzle #38
ACROSS
  1. 8/25; eight
  4. 18/25; eighteen
  5. 2/5; two
  7. 9/10; nine
  8. 1/5; one
DOWN
  1. 11/20; eleven
  2. 7/10; seven
  3. 3/10; three
  5. 12/25; twelve
  6. 1/4; one

Puzzle #39
ACROSS
  3. 68.74
  5. 14.883
  7. 59.5
  8. 69.874
  9. 286.674
DOWN
  1. 20.45
  2. 181.576
  3. 6.384
  4. 48.19
  6. 97.21

Puzzle #40
ACROSS
  1. 18.1
  4. 20.324
  6. 6.404
  8. 26.5
  9. 5.184
10. 249.84
11. 41.64
DOWN
  1. 15.3
  2. 6.826
  3. 30.454
  5. 26.728
  6. 6.454
  7. 229.81
  8. 24.05